T0063492

THE CAGED EAGLE

Inspiration for the Journey,
A SHORT STORY SERIES

VICKI L. THOMPSON

WESTBOW
PRESS®
A DIVISION OF THOMAS NELSON
& ZONDERVAN

Copyright © 2023 Vicki L. Thompson.

All rights reserved. No part of this book may be used or reproduced by any means, graphic, electronic, or mechanical, including photocopying, recording, taping or by any information storage retrieval system without the written permission of the author except in the case of brief quotations embodied in critical articles and reviews.

This book is a work of non-fiction. Unless otherwise noted, the author and the publisher make no explicit guarantees as to the accuracy of the information contained in this book and in some cases, names of people and places have been altered to protect their privacy.

WestBow Press books may be ordered through booksellers or by contacting:

WestBow Press
A Division of Thomas Nelson & Zondervan
1663 Liberty Drive
Bloomington, IN 47403
www.westbowpress.com
844-714-3454

Because of the dynamic nature of the Internet, any web addresses or links contained in this book may have changed since publication and may no longer be valid. The views expressed in this work are solely those of the author and do not necessarily reflect the views of the publisher, and the publisher hereby disclaims any responsibility for them.

Any people depicted in stock imagery provided by Getty Images are models, and such images are being used for illustrative purposes only. Certain stock imagery © Getty Images.

Scripture quotations marked NKJV are taken from the New King James Version®. Copyright © 1982 by Thomas Nelson. Used by permission. All rights reserved.

Scripture quotations marked BBE are taken from the Bible in Basic English. Public Domain.

ISBN: 978-1-6642-7773-1 (sc)
ISBN: 978-1-6642-7772-4 (e)

Print information available on the last page.

WestBow Press rev. date: 08/29/2023

In Honor of Brother, Father, Grandfather, and
Great Grandfather endearingly called Pawpaw,
a Fisherman

"Give Comfort, Give Comfort,
To My People,
Says Your God."

Isaiah 40:1
The Bible In Basic English

CONTENTS

FOREWORD

Our Lifetime entails a Journey of many highs and lows; Pathways of long and lonely desert stays wanting gentle words of encouragement to quench the pain;

Pensive walks through valleys, comforted by the presupposed strength of stalwart mountains, towering alongside;

Each is a blessing in its own way.

However, most valuable of all blessings is, similar to Moses's reaching the mountaintop.

A designation for perspective transformation, and a time of fellowship, in the midst of the Glory of it all.

Entrance into the new decade has been a series of solemn plateaux, encompassing deserts of confusion, and valleys of heartbreak, and loss.

Yet, dichotomously of introspection, redirection as well as reconnection to what matters most in this life, God and oneself and family and friends.

Grateful to God for my family, whom he predetermined our need for one another; Appreciating more, each's gift of God's peculiar touch.

Blessed by everyone's sharing of love, prayers, and encouragement.

For the spiritual guidance from my parents, my father a devout servant who has gone home to Glory and my mother whose quiet wisdom speaks loudly into listening ears as well as clergy ministering near and afar.

GOD,
Meticulously Formed Every Creature,
Unique And Purposeful.

PART ONE

MAGNIFICENCE OF AN EAGLE

Have You No Knowledge Of It?
Has It Not Come To Your Ears?
The Eternal God, The Lord,
The Maker Of The Ends Of The Earth,
Is Never Feeble Or Tired;
There Is No Searching Out Of His Wisdom."

Isaiah 40:28
The Bible In Basic English

Have you ever thought about the magnificence of an Eagle?

Well, I hadn't!

Other than, it being an endangered species at one time.

That is, until I received a phone call from my brother.

Early one morning, Pacific Standard Time, my telephone rang. I thought it was the usual Saturday morning, get your weekly update about the family call from my mother, but it wasn't.

It was my brother with whom I hadn't talked for years, not for any particular reason other than distance. He moved to the South.

Surprised, yet more than happy to hear from him. But as we began to share the usual niceties of catching up, my brain began uploading memories of the past.

Paul, my brother, the oldest sibling in the family, however, I never called him my big brother because he wasn't necessarily big or tall.

Abruptly, he interrupted my memory's replay, saying "I'm training to become a volunteer firefighter."

Wow, that's good news!

How is that going?

"I'm almost finished," he continued nonchalantly, then as if switching channels blurted, "last Sunday, I went to the zoo."

For a moment, those words hung in the air waiting for me to snatch them.

Instead, I tightened my grip on the phone, holding it closer to my ear, wondering its connection with firefighter training.

But before I could respond, he resumed saying, "I stayed there all day watching an eagle."

PART TWO

THE EAGLE'S UNIQUENESS

Created To Endure
The Most Fiercest Of Elements.

"He Gives Power To The Feeble,
Increasing The Strength Of Him
Who Has No Force."

Isaiah 40:29
The Bible In Basic English

Hearing the anxiousness in my brother's voice, I knew, I needed to listen to all that he had to say.

However, memories resumed uploading.

Paul, a peacemaker generally quiet, always smiling, yet would wince looking at the bunch of us, whenever Dad reminded him of his responsibilities as the eldest.

A memory forever etched in my heart, is of our parents beaming when he was hired by a highly regarded drafting company at the age of seventeen.

It was the mid-sixties, a young American family growing up in the era when the "Land of the Free" was crying out for freedom.

Across America, protests painted the landscape of the nightly news.

Vivid images colorized the grayscale monotone on black and white televisions of every household in the country.

Armed guards, beating and arresting peaceful protesters, shackled, after being hosed down by the blunt forces of fire hoses.

The anguish of black faces, smeared with Freedom's cry.

Rich heirs and heiress protesting against the rudiments of the status quo, abandoning mother and father to join the freedom of love and peace, a promised liberty of the Hippie's lifestyle.

Women, waving their bras in symbolic liberty, birthed the feminist movement.

Protesters garnered momentum from every airing of the nation's plight.

Each night, we sat and watched with mom and dad, tensed but comfortable, living in the suburbs far from the struggle, yet drawn near by the zeal of descriptive news reporters.

Paul, the youngest as well as the only Black in the company who wore a white shirt, *short-sleeved*, and a tie and dress slacks.

Other Blacks employed were identified by uniforms of the kitchen or cleaning staff.

One evening, for some reason, we all gathered just as Dad was giving him a new drafting toolset along with a pocket protector for his drafting pens.

Can you imagine our mom's and dad's chests sticking-out?

Paul, worked there only for a short time.

"Hey," he exclaimed.

"Are you listening?"

"I spent the whole day watching this particular Eagle."

Oh?

Why?

What was it doing?

His answer was slow and methodical, pronouncing the words, "It was in a Cage."

A Cage?

Perplexed, questions continued pouring out.

What do you mean in a cage?

This day and age?

How can an eagle be kept in a cage?

Shouldn't the Zookeepers keep it somewhere natural to its habitat?

PART THREE
THE EAGLE'S REIGN

Nestled At Rest
Atop
A Giant Redwood Tree
Swaying In The Wind
Or
Regally Perched,
High
On The Edge Of
A Mountainous Cliff.

"Let Your Eyes Be Lifted Up On High,
And See:
Who Has Made These?
He Who Sends Out Their Numbered Army:
Who Has Knowledge Of All Their Names:
By Whose Great Strength,
Because He Is Strong In Power,
All Of Them Are In Their Places."

Isaiah 40:26
The Bible In Basic English

Paul though smart, never competed for A's in school, yet was always the cheerleader in the background whenever our parents boast about our grades.

Months later, while at the dinner table a discussion about his job came up.

Sudden silence, as all eyes looked upon him, until Dad spoke saying, "I guess they didn't want a real man."

The subject never came up again, because we knew Dad understood, having served in the US Army, as an Artillery Specialist, a decade earlier.

"The Cage was opened," my brother mumbled softly.

Adjusting my seat, What?

What do you mean, opened?

"The top of the Cage was open," he repeated.

Then as if, I should have understood, he restated, this time much louder, "There wasn't any top on the Cage!"

Chuckling under my breath, If so. . . Why didn't it fly away?

PART FOUR

EAGLE'S UNPARALLELED STRENGTH

Claws,
Are Strong As Steel
Designed To Close
Like A Clamp
To Hold
Its Prey
Hundred Times Its Weight,
Inflight.

"Even The Young Men
Will Become Feeble And Tired,
And The Best Of Them
Will Come
To the end of his strength"

Isaiah 40:30
The Bible In Basic English

Life would have it that Paul and I returned to our birthplace near the same time.

I never knew much else about my brother, he married and soon was drafted into the army.

I went away to college, only returning home for holidays and short vacations.

But it was when we came full circle, he began to say to me, smiling, "You will always be my little sister."

Small town USA, some would consider in the Heartland, but portions of our family's heritage supplanted here long ago, when it was part of territories of Spain.

He began working for a hospital, day-shift cleaning staff. But his uniform was undistinguishable from other workers, except of course the medical staff. He seemed to be part of of the hospital's hosts, intuitively appearing to welcome us whenever we visited, and alerting us whenever a relative presumably, was admitted to the into the hospital.

Often sharing, whenever getting paid, sometimes unexpectedly, he would show up for visits at a cousin's house, grinning his arms filled with groceries.

During one of these visits, while we were chatting, he stated smiling, "I know the Lord," reached in his pocket, and pulled out a Psalms-New Testament Bible.

Then stated further, "I give these to people, I meet in the hospital."

I could feel his joy resting in his eyes that he had accepted the Lord, Jesus Christ, and the truths of God's Grace, the Liberty of His forgiveness and everlasting life.

Smiling, he handed the Bible to me.

It was a warm summer evening, he was wearing a short sleeved shirt, and as I reached to accept his gift, a silent gasp came from within me.

Stunned, my eyes widen, so to latched on to another explanation, other than what I was seeing.

Keloid marks ran down his arm covering where veins once were.

No other explanation entered my mind.

Instead, hearing the voice from within say, *heroin* then *silent suffering.*

Being hopeful, I took another quick glance, searching for fresh needle marks, gladly there were none, only old wounds.

PART FIVE

EAGLE'S WINGS

Imagine,
An Eagle's Wings
Its Length,
Its Breadth
And
Its Width.

"But those
who are waiting
for the Lord
will have new strength;
they will get wings like eagles:"

Isaiah 40:3la,
The Bible in Basic English

Watching Paul participate in many sports, although playing basketball, he seemingly preferred quiet, one-on-one competitions.

Surprised one day, when he showed me a valuable chess set that he secretly saved money to purchase.

Sitting in our high school gymnasium, noticing my brother being the only black kid competing in wrestling, and he was good at it.

Recalling, the first time he wore his Lettermen's sweater that are parents sacrificed to purchase, but Paul was determined to get the prestigious jacket which he was awarded later for sportsmanship.

So then, the Eagle was chained, some how?

"No it wasn't, he rebutted, there weren't any chains in the Cage."

What?

I asked, what do you mean?

More questions began to rattle, how did they keep him in the Cage?

There must have been some sort of invisible forcefield or something like that?

Wasn't there?

"No, there wasn't," he whispered.

"I sat, all day wondering the same thing.

So, I got up, walked, and touched the Cage.

"Then suddenly, the strangest thing happened, standing at the Cage.

The Eagle began looking at me as if understanding my thoughts then began slowly spreading out its wings."

That's when I saw it ..."

When he paused, I quickly asked, saw what?

"His Wings!"

His wings?

Quickly, he shouted back, "His Wings Were Clipped!"

Astonished, clipped?

What are you talking about?

I mean, why would they do something like that?

Thoughts flooded my mind at his silence, thinking, if so, shouldn't his wings heal overtime?

Or, do they keep clipping them like over-grown nails?

Then my mind's chatter stopped.

Silenced by life's reality.

There is more to it!

PART SIX

PERCEPTION OF THE EAGLE'S EYESIGHT

Knowing Intuitively To Wait
For The Right Moment
In The Wind
Before Launching
Into The Sky.

"See,
The Lord God Will Come
As A Strong One,
Ruling In Power:
See,
Those Made Free
By Him Are With Him,
And Those Whom
He Has Made Safe
Go Before Him."

Isaiah 40:10
The Bible In Basic English

Shortly after Dad went home to be with the Lord, Paul became seriously ill. Diagnosed initially having Vertigo but nothing seemed to remedy the symptoms. He was referred to another hospital, but the illness persisted.

After several more tests, he received an official diagnosis, having a medical condition containing so many letters it was unpronounceable.

So, he asked the doctor for an explanation.

Simply put, Paul was exposed to an high level of radiation, the prognosis, bone marrow transplant.

Interestingly, the year prior, Paul was promoted to a position in the surgery room. He was responsible for cleaning and preparing operating rooms before and after surgery.

His health deteriorated quickly after the second diagnosis.

Mom prayed, just wanting Paul home.

PART SEVEN

EAGLE SOARING

"They Shall Run,
And
Not Be Weary
They Shall Walk,
And
Not Faint"

Isaiah 40:31c
The Bible King James Version

An Amazing Adventure engaging a private transport for the two hundred mile journey.

The Lord's hand was evident in the process.

We were connected to a provider in Louisiana, not only would the company provide transportation north to veterans hospital then turnaround two hundred miles south.

The company just kept saying, "Yes, we can do this" and "Yes, we can do that."

More so, we asked, if they would accept a check over the phone, they responded politely, "No problem" and "Yes, we can do that."

Monday, three months after the last diagnosis, the private medical transport drove up to our family's home.

Paul, having renewed strength, nearly jumped from the gurney, seemingly leaping as he walked, while his firstborn daughter followed close behind. He smiled when reaching the front door, and stepped through its entrance, his arms raised, proclaiming;

"Mom, I made it home!"

THE EAGLE SOARING

On the wings of the wind
in the open terrain

Freedom's Journey

Amidst
the blue abyss
of the
Limitedless
Sky

PRAYER OF COMFORT

Heavenly Father, we pray your comfort for whomever has suffered in life's journey to hold on and hold-on to the truths of the liberty of the freedom which your Son, the Lord Jesus Christ has made us free.

And will receive your peace and strength in circumstances of suffering, hardships as well as loss of loved ones by understanding His Lordship over all things.

And will believe in His Work on the Cross which released us from the former bondages and plagues of this present life and world.

And proclaim now, the freedom of the Gospel of God's Grace; Righteousness, Forgiveness, and Mercy.

And will understand the liberality on which we hold in this new life, lived eternally in Christ, and anchors us in the abundance of the Glory of His Joy, overwhelmingly given for sacrifices of a surrendered life to Him.

In Jesus Christ's name

Amen

THE AUTHOR
VICKI L. THOMPSON

After, 25 years aspiring in a banker career, I answered the Call of the Lord and surrendered my life to Jesus Christ.

Several years later, I resigned from my employment.

Soon there after, my life was transitioned to unfamiliar and uncertain circumstances of the living in the South.

A place of old traditions, family positions and social economic hardships based upon the ideology of skin color despite family heritage.

Through which I learned to trust in the abundance of God.

Also, it was a place and time of great suffering having witnessed the passing of our Father, all of his remaining siblings, all of our Mother's sisters, and the unexpected passing of our Brother at the age of sixty-four, a year after our Father. Soon following, the sudden passing of our 2nd eldest Brother, and many cousins, aunts and uncles great and small.

However, the experience of suffering Loss and serving the bereaved, enables me to joyfully share the wonders of the

Life which awaits us in the Glory of God the Father, where his Son, Jesus Christ sits on the throne.

Now, I am a servant proclaiming the message of the Gospel of Jesus Christ through Evangelism, Inspirational Writings and Songs;

AUTHOR'S WORKS

Host, You, Life and God Podcast, conversations pertaining to life and a relationship with God in Jesus Christ based upon biblical principles.

You, Life and God Podcast is available on Podcast, Music and Radio stations

The Seed, the Concrete and the Source, 2nd Ed., *Inspiration for the Journey, a Short Story series,* no 1., Independent publication, Kindle Direct Publishing, 2019.

Article, "the Seed, the Concrete and the Source," featured on website, 2018.